OM NAMAH SHIVAYA

THE POWER OF OM

Meena Bhojwani

BALBOA.
PRESS
A DIVISION OF HAY HOUSE

Balboa Press books may be ordered through booksellers or by contacting:

Balboa Press
A Division of Hay House
1663 Liberty Drive
Bloomington, IN 47403
www.balboapress.com
1-(877) 407-4847

Because of the dynamic nature of the Internet, any web addresses or links contained in this book may have changed since publication and may no longer be valid. The views expressed in this work are solely those of the author and do not necessarily reflect the views of the publisher, and the publisher hereby disclaims any responsibility for them.

The author of this book does not dispense medical advice or prescribe the use of any technique as a form of treatment for physical, emotional, or medical problems without the advice of a physician, either directly or indirectly. The intent of the author is only to offer information of a general nature to help you in your quest for emotional and spiritual well-being. In the event you use any of the information in this book for yourself, which is your constitutional right, the author and the publisher assume no responsibility for your actions.

Any people depicted in stock imagery provided by Thinkstock are models, and such images are being used for illustrative purposes only.
Certain stock imagery © Thinkstock.

Printed in the United States of America

ISBN: 978-1-4525-6786-0 (sc)
ISBN: 978-1-4525-6785-3 (e)

Library of Congress Control Number: 2013901911

Balboa Press rev. date: 03/19/2013

I dedicate this book to my mom and our angel, Shivani.

Thank you, thank you, thank you.

Om.

Thank you, Joey, for converting my manuscript into Microsoft Word. Thank you, Adriane, for meeting me and finalizing the book with me. Thank you to all the people at Balboa Press for helping with the book.

Thank you, thank you, thank you.

Om.

Om
Om Namah Shivaya

O M IS A SACRED FORM in most religions. "The goal that all the Vedas declare, that all austerities aim at, and that men desire when they lead the life of continence … is om. This syllable om is indeed Brahman. Whosoever knows this syllable obtains all he or she desires. This is the best support; this is the highest support. Whosoever knows this support is adorned in the world of Brahma-Katha Upanishad 1. Om is one of the oldest and most widely known mantras.

An ancient text says om, also known as aum, is the sound of the universe. Om is a sound from which all the other sounds are created. Om is the sound of all the sources of energy. Om is the root mantra from which all the other mantras emerge. Om is used in chants and meditation. Om is a one-word mantra that is regarded as the supreme one. It is effective when recited physically, mentally, and spiritually.

Om connects you to the world through its vibrations, which again through vibrations connect you to the universe. Om is a meditation chanted by spiritual sages and yogis from Vedic times until the present day. Hearing om, saying om, and chanting om brings positive vibrations and protects you from the lower energies around you.

Chapter 1

Writing Om

WRITING OM REPEATEDLY WILL CONVINCE you and your divine mind to accept who you really are and what you really want out of life. Writing om will speed up the process of getting whatever you want in your life. Writing om will create positive vibrations in your life. Writing om will help you correct what is uncorrected in your life. You create what you deserve by writing om.

Later in this book there is a series of daily pages. One page says "Om" at the top. The opposite page says, "Miracles of Writing Om." Start writing om on the pages headed "Om." Write it as many times as you like. Pour your feelings out on the page as you write om. On the page headed "Miracles of Writing Om," write down any outcomes you see as a result of writing om. Write what you affirmed for and how many days you saw results by writing om.

Chapter 2

Saying Om

Writing and saying om in all circumstances—difficult or happy—will get you through life. That is the power of om. If things go well in our life, do we thank God at once? No. But if things are bad in our life, the first words we often say are, "Oh, God." So in situations good or bad, keep saying om. I am about to tell you how.

Make it a point to start your day by saying om. Begin as soon as you get up in the morning. Instead of greeting your family and friends with "Good morning," say "Om." Instead of saying "Good afternoon," say "Om." "Good evening," say "Om." And at the end of the day, say "Om," instead of "Good night."

Throughout the day, ask yourself how many times you say hi or hello. Instead of saying "Hello," or "Hi," say om, at least with your family members. For those who cannot say om at work, say om in your mind when using more traditional greetings. In this way, you do not miss saying om.

Saying om keeps our mind calm and at peace. It frees us from worries and mental stress. Saying om gives us true happiness. Saying om will let us live more easily in all the situations we face in our lives. Say om when you want something. If you are unhappy, say om. Say om when healing your body. If you want to heal any part of your body, keep your hand on the third eye (located between your eyes on the forehead) and say om as many times as you like.

Saying om can heal a headache. Saying om can also cure severe illness. I believe in this, and so will you when you start saying om throughout the entire day. Believe in it; you are not far away from a miracle then. Miracles do happen. Say om if you are stressed. Say om when you are angry, and you will see how quickly you calm down. Say om if you have mood fluctuations.

You will be able to control your divine mind when you say om. Saying om enables you to remove negativity from your mind, which is the actual cause of all problems and suffering. By saying om, you will experience only peace. By now, you must have realized how many times you have said om while reading this far. I am positive you must have gotten some inner peace by saying om.

How I started to say om is in the next chapter. It will amaze you how many more times you can say om in a day.

OM
OM NAMAH SHIVAYA

Chapter 3

Me and Om

MY NAME IS MEENA MAHENDER Bhojwani. I reside in Dubai, UAE. I live with my husband, my daughter, and my son. My son is a child with special needs. I do a lot of reading on autism (books, articles, e-mails, and autism files). I regularly go to bookstores to buy books on autism. One day, for no reason at all, I picked up Louise L. Hay's book *You Can Heal Your Life*. I kept this together with my other books for six months. Every time I picked up the book to read it, for some reason, I would put it back.

Like everyone else, I also had good and bad days. One night during a phase of bad days, I started reading this book and was awake the whole night reading it. In those days, I was suffering from unbearable heel pain in my left food. After having blood tests, X-rays, and many other tests, the doctor could not diagnose the problem. I was given painkillers and told to come back for more tests in a few days. I decided to stop the painkillers and started doing affirmations for my left heel. I read and wrote my affirmations every day for three months. I was healed in three months, and my left heel has been pain-free for over two years.

I read a lot of books by Louise L. Hay, and I started healing my family through affirmations. Yet I was not satisfied with what I was doing. I felt something was missing. One night while going through my mail, I got an e-mail about angel books by Doreen Virtue. I started reading about angels and also attended a workshop on how to connect with angels. For over a year now, I have done affirmations and called on angels to cure my family of colds, coughs, and headaches, as well as to keep us safe when traveling and other aspects of our lives. Yet, I still felt something missing.

I believe in all the gods, and for my son, I believe in Lord Shiva (Har Har Mahadev). I read for three to four hours a day. So I decided to start reading by saying om every day. For all the full stops in a sentence, I say om. So you can imagine in how many times I say om in three to four hours of reading. If I am saying affirmations, I say om after very sentence instead of full stop. If I call on the angels, I say om after I complete my sentence. If I am reading any articles or books on autism, after very sentence, I say om. I hope you can apply this theory in your life as well.

OM
OM NAMAH SHIVAYA

Chapter 4

Meditating Om

MEDITATING OM RELAXES THE MIND and maintains a healthy balance between your inner and outer worlds. Meditating om helps to keep your mind calmer and more focused. Meditating om can transfer your mind from negative mode to positive mode, from being upset to calm, from being unhappy to happy, from not knowing your mind to understanding your mind. Overcoming negative thoughts is the purpose of meditating om. Once you have overcome your negativity, your mind will be peaceful.

As you master the technique of meditating om, which is different for everyone, your mind will be freed from all worries, and you will be able handle all situations of your life. As for me, I can meditate om at any time of the day. I am a short-tempered person by nature, but meditating om has calmed me to a certain extent. But that does not mean I have mastered meditating om. No! It takes a lot of practice and patience to relax your mind and control your breathing.

With the increasing demands of life, we are stressed and overtired. I personally feel twenty-four hours is not enough to get everything done in a single day. All this stress can even affect our health. So let's make it a habit of meditating om for at least ten to twenty minutes every day.

Let's start our journey toward inner peace and calmness.

METHOD OF MEDITATING OM

Set a fixed time in your daily routine to meditate om. Unlike me, as I wrote earlier, I can meditate om at any time of the day. You can start your day with meditating om or meditating om in the middle of the day, or end your busy day by meditating om. Find a quiet, relaxing environment. Sit on level ground. Concentrate on your breathing and meditating om, silencing your mind completely.

Do whatever you feel is best for you. A method that works for you would not necessarily work for others. After a lot of practice, I found my method of meditating om. I hope you find your own method soon.

Based on my experience, the practice of meditating om should be done with great devotion. I meditate om in the morning or evening for an hour or more. When sitting down to practice my daily mantra om, I first chant om on my japa mala, given to me by my mother. It's a string with 109 beads on it. As I finish my japa mala, I don't let the meditation end. I keep chanting om loudly until I illuminate my angel tea light and place it in front of me, along with Lord Shiva's idol. Then, closing my eyes, I visualize a red light pouring through the crown chakra and reaching the root chakra, located at the base of the spine. I then visualize an orange light pouring through the crown chakra, reaching the hara chakra, located at the lower abdomen, genital area, womb. A yellow light pours through the crown chakra to the solar plexus chakra, located just above the naval. A green light pouring through the crown chakra reaches the heart chakra at the center of the chest. A light blue light pours through the crown chakra to the throat chakra, located at the center of the throat. Pouring through the crown chakra to the third eye chakra, located in the center of the forehead, is a light-blue light. A dark-blue light pours through the crown chakra and also reaches the third eye chakra. When a violet light pours into my crown chakra, I start meditating om, concentrating on my breathing and silencing my mind completely. If you have a problem in any part of your body, you can concentrate on that particular chakra and meditate.

OM NAMAH SHIVAYA
OM, OM, OM

OM
OM NAMAH SHIVAYA

Root Chakra—Balancing this chakra helps the central nervous system, muscular system, and skin.

Third Eye Chakra—Balancing this chakra helps the brain, neurological system, eyes, ears, and nose.

Throat Chakra—Balancing this chakra helps the throat, thyroid, esophagus, trachea, mouth, jaw, teeth, neck, and vertebrae.

Heart Chakra—Balancing this chakra helps the heart, circulatory system, ribs, breasts, lungs, shoulders, arms, and hands.

Solar Plexus Chakra—Balancing this chakra helps the stomach, pancreas, small intestine, liver, gallbladder, and middle spine.

Hara Chakra—Balancing this chakra helps the sexual organs, large intestine, pelvis, hips, and bladder.

Root Chakra—Balancing this chakra helps the spine, legs, bones, and feet. This chakra gives a lot of energy to the body.

Meditating all the chakras increases overall health.

OM
OM NAMAH SHIVAYA

Day 1

Day 2

Day 3

Day 4

Day 5

Day 6

Day 7

Day 8

Day 9

Day 10

Day 11

Day 12

DAY 13

Day 14

DAY 15

Day 16

Day 17

Day 18

DAY 19

Day 20

Day 21

Day 22

Day 23

Day 24

DAY 25

Om

Om Namah Shivaya

Please e-mail your experiences to me at meenabunty@
hotmail.com. Your stories will be published in
the next book to motivate other people.

ABOUT THE AUTHOR

MEENA BHOJWANI WAS BORN IN Mumbai, got married and settled in Dubai, UAE. Lives with her husband, daughter, and son. She is a certified Angel Therapist, Reiki Practitioner Level 1 and Qigong Practitioner Level 1.